MINDING THE SUN

Previous Books by Robert Pack

Minding
the Sun

Robert Pack

THE UNIVERSITY OF CHICAGO PRESS
Chicago and London

ROBERT PACK is College Professor of Literature and Creative Writing at Middlebury College. He is the author of three critical works and more than a dozen books of poetry, including *Fathering the Map: New and Selected Later Poems* (1993), also published by the University of Chicago Press.

The University of Chicago Press, Chicago 60637
The University of Chicago Press, Ltd., London
©1996 by Robert Pack
All rights reserved. Published 1996
Printed in the United States of America
05 04 03 02 01 00 99 98 97 96   1 2 3 4 5

ISBN: 0–226–64407–3 (cloth)
        0–226–64408–1 (paper)

Library of Congress Cataloging-in-Publication Data

Pack, Robert, 1929–
    Minding the sun / Robert Pack.
        p.   cm.
    I. Title.
PS3566.A28M56   1996
811'.54—dc20   95-31080
                                        CIP

∞ The paper used in this publication meets the minimum requirements of the American National Standard for Information Sciences—Permanence of Paper for Printed Library Materials, ANSI Z39.48-1984.

FOR PATTY
again and finally

CONTENTS

ACKNOWLEDGMENTS

The author wishes to thank the editors of the periodicals in which
the following poems were first published:

The American Scholar (Winter 1996): "Determination."
The Georgia Review (Summer 1994): "The Trees Will Die."
   Volume 48, no. 2.
The New Criterion (March 1994): "Observer."
The New Republic (November 6, 1995): "Circle."
Otter Creek Journal (Autumn 1994): "Panegyric for a Cockroach."
The Pacific Review: "Within Measure."
Prairie Schooner (Spring 1995): "Listening," and "Beyond Forgetting."
   Reprinted by permission of the University of Nebraska Press.
   Copyright 1995 University of Nebraska Press.
Shenandoah (Spring 1991): "The Human Eye."

ONE

THE PLACE

Here is the place—the house half hidden in dense pines,
The hill's slope rambling to the stream,
The swamp of jewelweed, the wild grape vines,
The vista of the valley like a red hawk's dream
Of floating steady on the wind ablaze
With orange light—and here, in silhouette, beyond
The hill's slope rambling to the stream,
Beyond the house half hidden in dense pines,
The mountain range recedes into blue evening haze;
Here is the place—the willow doubled in the pond
Where on a log two painted turtles gaze
At two suspended dragonflies above
A lily pad, like a reflected floating star—
Here's where we always will have been, my love;
Here is the place, here's where we were and are.

SUMMER

This is the full of summer, this is all
The bumblebee has ever dreamed about;
This is my rise that has no fall;
This is my in that has no out.
And this my body's happiness, the call
Of clover scented in the swaying air
The bumblebee has ever dreamed about.
This is the full of summer, this is all
Bold blossoming and blazing everywhere,
The hummingbird suspended at the rose
With no thought of your leaving in my mind.
This is my opening that has no close,
This is my now with nothing left behind,
No thought of winter thinking can't forestall;
This is the full of summer, this is all.

OCTOBER LINGERING

A blaze of orange in a blaze of red
As sunset lights the hillside sumac row;
This is the landscape suited for my head,
The mountain range above, the stream below,
And leisurely October lingering to wed
Its umber hues into a spreading glow
As sunset lights the hillside sumac row.
A blaze of orange in a blaze of red,
With yellow butterflies reposing everywhere
In circles by the puddles in the road,
Composes me in stillness so serene
I am diffused into the lilting air
As an abiding consciousness—as if the scene
Took pleasure in itself through me,
As if my substance had become transparency.

THE WAITING

Soft frost has settled on the boughs,
The maples brighten sunset red,
An uncollected bale of hay
Is all the stubble field allows
My thoughts to pause upon, to say
Once more what is already said:
The maples brighten sunset red,
Soft frost has settled on the boughs.
Three chickadees alight, and now
A maple welcomes them the way
Frost settles on the sunset boughs
And one abandoned bale of hay
Contains the stubble field, the way
My thoughts pause deeper into red,
The way I wait by saying what is said.

EGGPLANT

Responding to approval in your glance,
Your eggplant wonders if it is a god,
A local god one might find anywhere by chance
With no distinguishing or odd
Capacity for transformation or disguise,
And yet, despite its ordinary shape and size,
Your eggplant wonders if it is a god.
Responding to approval in your glance,
I and the other neighbor deities
Display our bounty of bold ripening—
Tomatoes, squash, green peppers, carrots, peas
Proclaim the blessing each of us can bring,
Demanding adoration here alone,
Dumb to your other realms of ripened trees,
Dumb to a summer bounty all your own.

LEAVING

As you left in a swirl of early snow,
The last I saw of you was your fur hat.
Your thinned lips hinted that you had to go;
Perhaps the slightness of a sign was what
I should have understood—just that
Receding look in your cold eyes. How could I know
The last I'd see of you was your fur hat
As you left in a swirl of early snow?
Now I envision you transformed into a fox,
Stalking among the junipers for mice—
As if your wish to try a different life
Were realized, so I'm not shocked
To watch you disappear into your den, although
My mind is swirling with the swirl of snow.

THE POND

A glaze of ice grips the hushed pond
Below the stone ledge where I sit to yearn,
Staring at the reflection of
The hazy sun, staring beyond
The cedar fence, the misted hemlock grove,
Hoping you will return.
Below the stone ledge where I sit to yearn,
A glaze of ice grips the hushed pond,
Squeezing it down into the pumpkin size
Of the reflected sun,
As if such dulled reflection helps me realize
The harvest of your being gone—
Harvest of emptiness beyond
Which there is no beyond, only the sun
Gripped in the ice grip of the hazy pond.

EMBELLISHINGS

Just sunrise glinting silver in the dew,
Just evening haze amid high pines,
These are my chosen messages to you,
These are my meanings, my designs,
As if beholding shaded shifts of light,
From blue embellishings to hues of gold,
Told everything that needed to be told:
Just evening haze amid high pines,
Just sunrise glinting silver in the dew.
For what is left to say except I'm here
To hold all blue embellishings in sight,
To watch gold hues dissolve and reappear
As morning brightens yellow into day,
As dusky evening darkens into night
With you away, my love, with you away.

LISTENING

Uncertain flute notes flutter in the stream,
Low hillside wind moans cello sounds;
With you away, I listen as they merge and seem
To form a pattern that astounds
The quaking leaves, connecting me to a design
Beyond my own designing as I realize
Low hillside wind moans cello sounds,
Uncertain flute notes flutter in the stream.
And though this music is not mine,
Without my improvising ears and eyes,
Only dumb wind and water fill this place,
Wind merely wind, and water with no cries
Reflecting the streaked weather in my face,
Until I hear an oboe rising from the dew,
With your blue absence there to listen to.

LOON CALLS

Come back and linger here a while!
Within the windy shade along the lake, two loons
Call out to welcome you,
As if to fill the silence of your absent smile
With music of my melancholy
And transform mourning into something new.
Within the windy shade along the lake, two loons
Come back and linger here a while
To pour out liquid melody
Where I still linger in an air your absence made,
Still wondering why have you gone
And left me with the loons in moody shade
My gloom can feast upon,
Consuming every whirling wind in view
That fills my emptiness which welcomes you?

NOVEMBER DAWN

How can I say what thunder used to say?
How can I make dark silence speak?
This foggy dawn in dim November light
A clump of leafless birch trees sway
Against a silhouetted cloud
That frowns into a face the way
Old angry thunder used to speak,
To say what whirlwinds used to say.
I hear a cardinal, not yet in sight,
Call to her mate; she whistles loud
Into the wind as if dark silence might—
Because that's how things happen to the weak—
Leap out and snatch his life away.
And still no voice from a condemning cloud
Says what the thunder used to say.

OWL REFLECTIONS

Looking into a moonlit forest pond,
I watch a white owl in my rippled face
Hunched in a hemlock tree, and I can trace
His glaring light way back beyond
The path you took and to the cloud
That blurs the snow-stilled mountain peak.
I watch a white owl in my rippled face
Looking into a moonlit forest pond
As if he were about to speak
To you my mourning words, as if his loud
And undulating hootings found
Some meaning in the undiscerning wind
That shakes my image in the pond
But cannot carry it beyond regret
Where you won't watch me watching yet.

THE WATCHER AND THE HAWK

The hawk floats in a thermal lift;
My mind enters itself and stares
Back at its own staring. As the hawk's drift
Circles its circlings, like an ancient sign
Inscribed in wind, which bares
No message I can designate as mine,
My mind enters itself and stares.
The hawk floats in a thermal lift
Until a rougher wind breaks loose
And brings tears to my unenlightened eyes,
Although I know I cannot choose
To let those tears—caused merely by the way
Wind slices in—rend meaning like a prize
From that hawk streaking down to snatch its prey,
As I stare at my staring this pure day.

SNOW RISE

Dreaming time has reversed, I watch drowned snow
Appear to lift up from the lake;
Reshaping magnified, each risen flake
Looms in the air, deliberate and slow,
Allowing me to let your picture form and wake
Astonished that you have returned to go
To watch me watch drowned snow lift from the lake.
Dreaming time has reversed—and you,
Your red cheeks radiant against the wind,
Are gliding toward me on the ice into
A frame of gilded twilight—I
Again awaken from your being gone to find
Your gloved hands covering your lips' *good-bye*
So you can watch me watch uplifted snow
As if your absence now concluded long ago.

STORM

Cascading snowflakes settle in the pines,
Sculpting each tree to fit your ghostly form
The surge of swirling wind defines
As if your human shape were what the storm
Sought to contrive, intending to express
Its consciousness of my white consciousness,
Sculpting each tree to fit your ghostly form.
Cascading snowflakes settle in the pines,
Swaying in unison beneath the snow,
Calling me to you with wild gesturings
Homeward into the howling woods, although
Thinking of your abiding spirit brings
Only a whiter absence to my mind,
Only whirled snow heaped up by whirling snow,
Only a fox whose den I cannot find.

MIDWINTER THAW

Stunned in their voiceless way to be alive
This drizzling three-day January thaw,
Green lilac buds appear that won't survive
When Arctic winds crack down from Canada
And half-starved foxes shake and paw
A rabbit carcass in its stiffened fur.
Green lilac buds appear that won't survive
This third day of our January thaw,
This gap in time, this season not their own,
Merely a mockery of spring
With sun's warmth wasted on a stone,
And still my mind goes groping in the mud to bring
Some stubborn sprouts up through the stubble hay,
To follow in the path of their brief blossoming
In search of brighter green to come. No way!

BETRAYAL

I moaned my lamentation out alone
When brute wind blasted through the underbrush
And split the ancient maple in a rush
Of icy snow, but not for sorrow of my own,
Not for betrayal by those friends who turned away
When I had no more favors to bestow
When brute wind blasted through the underbrush.
I moaned my lamentation out alone
Because the blizzard in my mind could say:
Pain is impersonal as February sleet,
As natural as winter in the bone
Or icicles descending from the eaves,
Transfiguring what causes it to be.
I am the griever who becomes the grief he grieves;
Betrayed, I am the ice, the wasted leaves.

FOX WOUND

Just as the lame fox peers out from her den,
I hear you in the pine woods, calling me.
This is the fox you rescued when
She was a wailing kit, her paw caught in a trap;
You nursed her for two months, then set her free,
And every year at mating time, I see
Her limp across the field again.
I hear you in the pine woods, calling me,
Just as the lame fox peers out from her den,
Just as a wind-split pine branch cracks
And crunches down, just as a ruffed grouse rushes,
Blurring past my face, and smacks
Headlong into the tangled underbrush.
But I am wrong, for you have not returned;
My wound remembers yours—with nothing learned.

THE WALL

The apple trees need pruning once again;
Spilled stones again need piling on the wall
I built to circle our new homestead when
I cleared the field and settled here with all
Eternity awaiting me so I can go
On being what I have become, to know
Spilled stones again need piling on the wall,
The apple trees need pruning once again.
Now that you're gone, though I can still recall
My sculpted trees, eternity is left behind—
The tangled branches crowd out their sparse light;
Stones crawl back to the scrub field in my mind
And burrow underground in the grim night
As if at home again, as if content,
As if a circling wall was never what they meant.

SPRING RETURNS

The willows flash their first faint hint of green—
Faint but arousing to this watcher's sight,
Greedy for color after winter white
That means what windy snow must mean
To one observing someone who's not there
And sees her absence lurking everywhere.
Faint but arousing to this watcher's sight,
The willows flash their first faint hint of green
As my numbed heart's resurging need for hope—
Earth's burgeoning in hues of April's sheen—
Startles my blood; I feel hope in the swoop
And easy uplift of the coasting hawk.
Yet nothing in the scene replaces her,
No softness in the air, no memory, no talk:
Grief grips me like a stiff, brown thistle burr.

SILENCE

As silence stretches out across the lake,
Except for when a yellow perch rips through
To snatch a fly, I rise up stark awake
At misty dawn as if I slipped into
Your windless realm of woven shade
With quietness the willow made
Except for when a yellow finch rips through.
As silence stretches out across the lake,
I breathe transparent peace, peace so impersonal,
Like air within blue air, for the last sake
Of finding self outside of self, the full
And final culmination of desire to free
Myself of all desire, even for you
In silent shade, except for when I see
A yellow perch, a yellow finch rip through.

CIRCLE

When I think *circle* I can choose the sun
As illustration, I can choose the moon,
Or, nearer home, I can imagine one
Unblemished orange shining in my hand,
And, shutting out the life behind me, soon
There's only *form* for me to understand:
As illustration, I can choose the moon
When I think *circle*, I can choose the sun.
Behind me is the long descent that led,
As smoothly as the settling of two butterflies
Upon a stone, to the acceptance that instead
Of holding on, I let you go—as if my eyes
Could close on memory, except for one
Last look at orange light to linger on,
Whose circle will remain when sun and moon are gone.

THE MERGING

Each you becomes another you—all one,
You separate and merge within my mind;
As wife, as mother, father, daughter, son,
You show a single face, so I can find
Or lose myself in every set of eyes I see,
And staring inward at the you in me
You separate and merge within my mind.
Each you becomes another you—all one,
Like leaves unfurling on a maple tree,
Or like reflected moonlight on a lake,
You seem uncertain being there,
You seem both sleeping and awake,
And staring inward at my inward stare,
I recognize you looking back to see
My vanished image in the vacant air.

HER SHOES

I watch her from the bottom of the stairs;
Her shoes reverberate with silver light;
She waits there for my father, unawares
I'm playing my toy trumpet on this rainy night
To celebrate their anniversary,
And though I don't know how they met, I see
Her shoes reverberate with silver light.
I watch her from the bottom of the stairs
And try to picture where they were
When blindly they conceived of me:
Beside a lake of drifting ducks that stir
The lily pads, beneath a willow tree
With wind that whips up silver waves for her,
The same suffusing silver as her shoes,
Smooth silver of my choice—for him to choose.

REUNION

So here you are at our old camping site
Where three streams meet to form a waterfall.
Why on your wedding anniversary tonight?
Why have you reappeared at all?
I'm old enough to be your father now,
Now that it's forty years since our last talks
Where three streams meet to form a waterfall.
So here you are at our old camping site
Reminding me there's art in how
One cleans a fish or swings an axe,
Or maybe after all these silent years
Your restlessness still seeks
To ask the meaning of your wife's remarried tears:
Would she return if you should call
Where three streams meet to form a waterfall?

TURTLES

The earth, one great green bucket, sits at ease
Upon a turtle's back, his bony head
Thrust out for balance in the cosmic breeze,
My vexed, gesticulating father said;
That turtle stands upon another turtle so
It's turtles infinite plus one that you can count
Each on another turtle's back, mount after mount.
The earth, one great green bucket, sits at ease
No matter how far down the turtles go,
No matter if some super bottom turtle brings
Itself into existence from the lake
Of his own mind, and then in silence sings
All other turtles into light for earth's green sake.
The grin you see on every turtle's face
Is proof, my father said, and paused to rest his case.

ONLY IN ZOOS

When the last elephants are locked in zoos,
When chimpanzees cohabit in a cage,
What bedtime stories will we parents choose
To tell our children as their thoughts still rage
For wild things romping over rocky streams?
What images will stir their dreams
When chimpanzees cohabit in a cage?
When the last elephants are locked in zoos,
And in the park, above the carousel,
Two cockatiels alight, escaped
From homes where they were fed and guarded well,
Not knowing that our winters here are shaped
By snow squalls in the spectral boughs; what will we tell
The untamed wind whose memory
Was bred when lightning struck the swirling sea?

THE SEA

The sea, the sea, the unrelenting sea!
Green vistas opening on openness
Evoke another self whom I might be
And send me soaring in a guess
Until the dark swerve downward of a cormorant
Across the hazed, half-risen sun distracts me from
Green vistas opening on openness.
The sea, the sea, the unrelenting sea
Revives my longing in the lifting fog; I can't
Restrain desire to wish beyond this shore-bound me,
Beyond the swish and swirl of curling waves that come
Undone upon the shell-strewn shore, and though it's true
Muted shore music still can soothe and bless,
Smooth wave sounds tide me out again into
Green vistas opening on openness.

LAUGHTER

I laughed my weirdest, wildest laughter out
Up to the stars, across the galaxy,
To let them wonder what such wildness was about,
Why such defiant laughter came from me—
A single soul beside a moonlit lake
Reflecting still on my expanding singleness
Up to the stars, across the galaxy.
I laughed my weirdest, wildest laughter out
With late owls swerving among hemlock trees
As if their hootings circled Venus, circled Mars,
Knowing the widened night would echo me
By filling every space between the stars,
Opposing silent emptiness,
With just me by an all-reflecting lake
Whose laughter multiplied my life for life's own sake.

NIGHT SWIM

So far away, you could not know,
Though you surmised what green force pulled me down,
That this was not the first night that I swam
Beyond your call, beyond the shore lights' glow
Whose quietude enwrapped your calm,
So far away, you could not know,
Though you surmised what green force pulled me down.
I think you lingered in my last intent
To leave you with a whispered guess
What my night swim, so far away, had meant—
My gliding with the outbound tide might still possess
Your swirling thoughts; my moonlit peace
Of spray and spume, my buoyant element
Also might be your spindrift, green release.

BEYOND FORGETTING

I don't know why I brought this gun;
I don't recall the killer whom I meant to kill
Now that I've journeyed farther from the sun,
Past Mars and Jupiter, now that my will
Can focus on my merging with the stars.
Now that I near the center of the Milky Way
And cannot see cold Jupiter and Mars,
I don't recall the killer whom I meant to kill.
I don't know why I brought this gun;
I don't know what I want to say
Of all I thought still needed to be said
To take leave of the living brotherhood
Of animals who never understood
The silent bullet entering their head.
Who will protect them now that I am dead?

HOMEWARD

Across the soft hum of galactic space,
I'm drifting homeward toward Andromeda;
My feet and my curled fingers whir
While orbiting around my face,
Returning from a lifetime on the earth below,
And so *good-bye* to that receding place,
I'm drifting homeward toward Andromeda.
Across the soft hum of galactic space,
I hear the dwindled warbling of an oriole
And smothered pebbles tumbling in a stream;
I see swirled mountain mist condensed to dew
Within an orchard wind, within a dream
Some other me is dreaming now of you,
Calling in tones that I can't recognize—
A face without your lips, without your eyes.

MINDING THE SUN

Although two million light-years there from here,
Still setting in my mind—I scan the Sun
Lighting its planetary sphere,
A small star in a common galaxy, not one
My dear, worth singling out except that we lived there,
And though it's time to let remembrance go,
Still setting in my mind—I scan the Sun.
Although two million light years there from here,
From spiraling Andromeda
Out to the Milky Way, and even if I know
It's time for last relinquishings, for her
Vast purple amplitude upon a mountaintop
To vanish wholly from my sight,
I think of swallows swooping through, and stop
Them faithful in their flight.

TWO

OBSERVER

Only a universe with an initial density exactly equal to critical density would be capable both of engendering motherly stars and of lasting long enough to provide a home for the nuclear, chemical, and biological reactions required for life to subsist.... This "fertile" density is the first condition any universe must meet before it can hope to produce its own observer.
—Hubert Reeves, *The Hour of Our Delight*

Muse of the universe,
muse of mass-energy, I'd never known
critical density
is a conception that I need
to take personally:

force of initial thrust required
for fiery particles to be propelled
without collapsing back because
the pull of gravity
could halt expansion and prevent the laws

that govern simple cooling
from engendering enduring stars.
Through improvising time,
mothering stars could then provide us
with a place where melody and rhyme,

in turn, would be conceived from
nuclear and chemical reactions,
from organic ooze.
I'd never known that metaphor
also required mothering, so that deep blues

can represent our gloom,
green can convey renewal, red evoke desire,
  and white betoken emptiness
or innocence because those primal particles
  designed us to express

what our initiating species has become—
  observers of the patient stars
    that mothered us to bear
true witness to the story of the past
  unfolding everywhere,

enabling us to apprehend the music
  of the whirling planets
    as they orbited the sun,
enabling us to feel the harmony
  fertile density had begun.

So here we are, observing with our eyes
    the slant light through the pines
  before the orange sun descends
behind the bluish-purple misted hills;
  and here we are as moonlight sends

    fresh flashings through the lake
and multiplies the silvery reflections
    while they slide and spill
  and merge with our own thoughts,
which cast their own reflecting light at will

as if the act of looking
added hue and aura to the night;
and here we are at dawn, here's why we came,
observing with our ears
the way the whip-poor-will repeats his name,

hearing the pulse of words
we have evolved to listen with,
observing with the mind
the mind's brave observations of itself,
enabling us to find

thought can engender from its own
critical density
a fertile universe through which to roam,
which metaphor, in blue or green
or red or white, can designate as home.

HUMMINGBIRD

Big Bang occurred against the odds
from nothingness, and contemplating chance
    of such gigantic magnitude
in his epiphanous and famous hunch,
    Al Guth, the physicist, remarked
"The universe may be the ultimate free lunch."
    "So you can chew on that awhile,"
        I pep-talk to myself,
    though I still hunger for some purpose
in blue silence of ancestral air
    whose whitened noontime radiance
        seems to reply to me
    with its reflections on your hair
as you, composed within the window frame,
    stand staring at a hummingbird.
Her wings seem manifest as liquid light
        as if they will dissolve
    this whirring instant in your sight
into the nothingness from which they came
    some fifteen billion years ago.
But now she sips the secret dew that lies
    within each petal's purple glow
that streams out from the basket of impatiens
        that her minuscule beak
    will visit daily at this hour
        until broad summer ends,
until you are no longer here to watch
    and mirrored nothingness commends

my absent-minded thoughts for thinking absence
      is so palpable that I
can taste it like ripe fruit upon my lips.
      And now I see you in the room
          you have already left;
I see the hummingbird just as she sips
      the succulent sweet nectar
even though she is no longer there;
          I see her held in place
by wings that beat so fast that they create
          an opening in space
      from which this breathless noon
she can breathe forth or she can disappear
          like my willed thoughts of you,
      composed within the window frame
where blue returns to white and white to blue.
          As long as I imagine
      nothingness, palpable absence
in the room tempts me to make my next command,
          and I can conjure you
beside the window, staring at a hummingbird,
          an apple in your hand.

THE HUMAN EYE

Although the belief that an organ so perfect could have been formed by
natural selection, is enough to stagger any one; yet in the case of any organ,
if we know of a long series of gradations in complexity, each good for its
possessor, then, under changing conditions of life, there is no logical impossi-
bility in the acquirement of any conceivable degree of perfection through
natural selection.—Charles Darwin, *The Origin of Species*

No miracle was needed to preserve
      our sightless ancestors.
Salt tears replaced the primal sea that then
    protected their emerging eyes
which first found form by chance mutation when

    the membrane on an eye-pit thickened
to become a lens. Selection took its time to shape
    the human eye, which can perceive
the roundness of a drop of dew composed
      upon a willow leaf

as if the concept, roundness, could itself
    be held in focused thought,
could be possessed and thus be seen
    as something round, complete,
    returning to itself as green—

    reflected in the dew—
  becomes more green, turns greener still,
staggers my mind with greenness. Now the sun—
    hazy at dawn, not yet
too blinding bright to gaze upon in one

prolonged look at its circled light—
enters the green world of the dew, becomes
         pure liquid roundness, ripe
     as in the idea of perfection
that my mind beholds before a blink will wipe

     the round world back to shapeless darkness
        those first eyes were rescued from
through each gradation in complexity.
       It's possible, the thought
of such a series staggers me

      with awe, astonishment,
as if it were a miracle, as if
     time were itself a miracle,
changing conditions for the good of change
    so that the law of natural

      selection could inspire
the adaptation to survive, with each change good
     for its possessor—me. It's mine,
this good of sight: I see the dawn wind shift
    the green to silver in the pine

outside my door beyond my touch; I see black wings
    flash white as one rose-breasted grosbeak
      startles from the silver shade.
I see now that I see my own desire to see,
    as if each bird, each leaf, were made

so I can reach beyond
what I can touch, and thus conceive
newly acquired conception going on
gradation by gradation as
new ripeness takes the place of ripeness gone

for good, and that's good for the new
possessor—me! And now, before I sleep,
before my salty eyes return
to the originating dark our ancestors
were rescued from, I yearn

to find completion in the flare of green,
watching dew spill from a stirred leaf
this silver moment in the hazy sun
as if my eyes survive
to see myself in seeing everyone.

ROOTING FOR PLEASURE

for Bob Hill

You say, Charles Darwin, that
"the sense of beauty in its simplest form
            was first acquired when certain
      colors, sounds, and forms gave pleasure
to the lower animals." Now that's the norm
      for human looking at a flower—
            let's say, chrysanthemum.
What gaudy pleasure just to gaze
upon its layered petals, gold on gold,
            emerged from morning haze,
surrounding central disks of denser gold,
            those greedy imitations
of the autumn sun. Its color, yellow,
      and repeating circles as its form
            together make a mellow
combination in the quickened air.
      The name, mellifluous in sound,
            merges with the moist smell
of baled hay in the lifting breeze.
Bold yellow beckons me, although I cannot tell
      what renders it agreeable
beyond the flower's purpose to survive,
      as if it flourished through desire
to offer beauty, consolation, hope,
            to meet a human need,
its petals mimicking the random fire
      of leaping sunbursts made symmetrical,

not for possession or for use, only
for us to contemplate.
I wonder how our wonder was acquired,
who was the pauser first to wait
beside a clover field,
holding his other hungers back, to watch—
not reaching bodily to touch—
a form emerging yellow from the mist,
until, in one great rush, so much
he's freed to feel leaps out that for an instant
he becomes the certain form
he dwells upon. Chrysanthemum,
I taste its tangy name as if it were a peach,
the murmured "m"'s, the hum
of its last, rounded syllable,
vibrating like the root note of a triad
as my seasoned sense evokes
the rough of peach fuzz on my greeting lips
to counterpoint the flavor's strokes
of sweetness on my tongue.
How did it start, such pleasure
to no end but to redouble my delight,
as if each dawning instant woke
eternity unfolding at a glance—twin sight
of colored form, of symmetry,
repeating circles mimicking the sun,
evolving with the name,
khrusanthemon, from the Greek root.
A radical departure from mere sight,
my flower does not look the same
as when the world was singly what it was,

unrescued by our naming sense
that learned to pluck, with any random breeze,
    prestidigitated pleasure
from ripened, newly knowledgeable trees,
      which seemed, ah, suddenly
  to need our praise, so that our names
for all forms perishable then could find
      each one of us still rooted
  in awe's golden light, reflecting
on the shimmering reflections of the mind.

PANEGYRIC FOR A COCKROACH

for Mariane Howard

What does success feel like,
set in the first design you hit upon
    250 million years ago?
By now you must assume you've learned the trick
    of immortality; you know
however random circumstances change,
    you'll improvise a strategy
for modern cockroaches to stay the same.
      Content with what you are,
    you know the accolades of fame,
as written by Lord Cockroach up above,
    will go to those who learned
that innovation's goal is to maintain,
    with minor variations, happy
creatures in their happy form. Since there's no gain
    in improvised complexity,
leading to self-awareness, worth the loss
    of stable steadiness,
you are not driven by the hungry need
    to wish, to pray, to curse, to bless,
      just your ancestral homes
under old logs or in loose bark of trees,
      decaying vegetables
      or the remains of animals,
    is all the dream of paradise that pulls
    you back to what you are.
Although you've colonized throughout the globe
    with flexibility of size,

you've always loved the safety of the night,
and you've been worldly wise
to keep your wings so they can fold
flat on your carapace, enabling you to hide
in crevices and cracks.
And yet your main adaptive change
to hold old evolution in its tracks
is to attach yourself
to human habitats like kitchens, bakeries,
and restaurants—all stores
where food abounds and lamps and pipes protect you
from the snow and rain. This flair of yours
to seek the easy life without remorse,
this gift to make yourself at home
in your own universe,
is what I envy and admire,
and since you take this world for better or for worse,
when a new comet strikes the earth,
like the last one that wiped out all the dinosaurs,
no doubt you will survive
that natural catastrophe.
And even if we manage to contrive
some new destruction of our own
by poisoning the waters
or by heating up the atmosphere,
your long experience will find
some new way to adapt—although I fear
our upstart species
of two million years will sink back down
again to fertilize the gasping dust
as your mute happiness moves on.
Though you can't think this for yourselves, I think
you'll miss us when we're gone.

THE TROLL BENEATH THE BRIDGE

"Filled with ancestral memories,"
the reptile brain within the old brain stem,
    asserts Professor Paul McLean,
lives like a wary troll beneath a bridge,
    obsessive, paranoid, and mean,
        and I can see his point
comparing trolls to lizards blinking in the sun,
    so locked in their compulsive ways
        of steady guardedness
    that they can doze away their days
        and still remain alert
to any hint upon the crackling air
    wet slashing teeth stalk them nearby.
And so they go on being what they were;
    maybe that is their doom, but I
        am not like them: my doom
is wholly different, for it's a fact
    we giant trolls are dying out—
the evidence is not just in my mind.
    Unless things change, there is no doubt
someday there'll be no trace of us; our caves
    will be inhabited by bears.
        Those scheming dwarf trolls hide
    behind the rocks and slaughter us
beside the drinking pools, because our pride
    won't let us band together to
protect ourselves, though we're three times their size.

I cannot comprehend
       their hatred of our kind—unless
they really do assume that in the end
       the earth belongs to them. You see,
it's natural that we retaliate,
       and I'll admit, in this regard
              we, too, are just like reptiles,
fixed in rigid memories too hard
       to alter, though I can
persuade myself we would be happier
       if all us trolls at last made friends.
I'm not afraid to tell those dwarfs,
       before the last thaw ends
and killing season starts next week,
       we can't go on like this.
Yet when I try to concentrate to speak,
       I can't be sure what words will soar
squawking out of my mouth like flapping crows
       who sullenly stare down
and watch me at a distance from their tree.
       Voices are in my blood—
       they speak to me, they speak *through* me,
but I'm confused by what they say. I'm crouched
       beneath this bridge because
someone thought he was chased by trolls and vouched
       he'd seen us loping down the hills,
someone with reptile ancestry, and thus
       with apprehensions of his own.
       Maybe he is the one,
       with dark lore deep within his bones,
I hear right now patrolling on the bridge
       he guards from someone in his head.
It makes no sense because that someone's *me*,
       though I am only what his fears
imagine what a giant troll must be.

Perhaps some creature able
to subdue the past will take my place
        because he knows the words that say
                who he has been, and is,
not moaning words that faintly fade away,
        dissolving in one long low howl
                that echoes in the cliffs
        beyond the riverbed below.
Perhaps he waits now, dreamless in the sun,
        deciding which brave way to go.

THE LOSS OF ESTRUS

Estrus must have been lost at some point in human ancestry. . . . When
hunting became a dominant male economic activity, perhaps the costs
(in terms of fitness) to females of constant sexual activity [due to the loss
of estrus] were outweighed by the benefits of receiving meat.
—Donald Symons, *The Evolution of Human Sexuality*

            Fertility is good—
        I want to multiply, and yet
without that fabled loss of estrus, dear,
        the wisdom of ancestral genes,
we'd now be making love three times a year.
        That really would be quite enough,
assuming I could get the timing right,
            unaided by the scent
        of ovulation in the air,
if replication of myself were all sex meant
        to me as a progenitor—just
an afternoon's hiatus from the hunt.
        I don't know what the cost
to you has been, but you look mighty fit to me,
        so I'll assume no zest is lost
            in all our huff-and-puffing,
spendthrift, sexual activity
        the loss of estrus—quite
    untypical of mammals—made
inevitable. Thus, establishing the right
        incentive for us males
to stick around, abandoned estrus set the stage
            for the invention of

a marital ideal of love
around the seasons. And more virtues
        followed from the first:
    as when one genius simian
        woke up and understood
    that a connection could be found
between his fornicating and his fatherhood.
        Nuzzling his nervous wife,
        he swore, "I'll bring meat home, my dear,
after our band completes the hunt; I vow
        that I'll stay faithful through this year
            and faithful when our kids
        leave home, and if familiar shadows
gliding through my silent dreams are true,
        even beyond the cramped-in grave
I'll rise to spend eternity with you."
        And so it must have been
with that light, evolutionary leap
        in self-persuading eloquence,
the world's first marriage vow was born;
        that's why it still makes sense
for us to look each other in the eye and say
        we'll redesign the creatures
that we are so we'll behave a better way
        than any mammal has before.
Despite your ancestor's low motive for romance,
        my dear, *protein deficiency,*
we'll now pretend the loss of estrus was
        your own transfiguring idea
            that captivated me,
        an idea that new vows of love
            might yet be built upon,
when my hot tooth for hunting flesh has cooled
        and all hormonal scents are gone.

LAMENT OF THE MALE GAMETE

Throughout animals and plants: the sex cells or "gametes" of males are much smaller and more numerous than the gametes of females. . . . This places a limit on the number of children a female can have. . . . Since she starts by investing more than the male, in the form of her large, food-rich eggs, a mother stands to lose more if the child dies than the father does.
—Richard Dawkins, *The Selfish Gene*

Now, I suspect, she's learned to be on guard!
        The gateway to the promised land
has been sealed off; I'm barred from entering.
        The writing on the wall proclaims—
"Abandon hope all ye who fumble here!"—
                and with these words that burn
into the echo cavern of my mind,
        my dread of barrenness returns;
                I shudder in the tumbling
of the crowded tide. Millions of years
        conspired to make me small for speed,
so I could thrash and swim without the fears
                of failure and of waste,
        willing to brave fantastic odds.
But now heroic effort is in vain—
        no force of mine can pierce this wall;
                I feel unprecedented pain
        in being cheated of the chance
to make myself into a multitude
                because my scent of her
that once unfailingly could seek her out,
                diminishes and fades.
        I'm left with just a swimmer's urge
among massed millions of competitors
                to stay afloat and bob about.

Yet I believe if I could merge
with her vast body, bountiful with food,
          unite with her alone,
I would remain with her, protect our brood,
          few though they are—unlike
     the stars reflected on the sea.
          Blind thrashing can't be all:
a mission to oblivion! There's got to be
     a hidden passage through this wall
               to where she waits for me.
My bruised head must be more than some grim sign
          of her newfangled wish:
     retaliation for old eons
          of my kind deserting her.
I need new inspiration to go on,
          bounce back and try again,
     to keep my head above the tide,
          triumphantly survive,
     like trilobites evolved to fish,
          like fish evolved to birds,
     like birds reformed to glowing men
of bodily perfection and ordained,
     cell by redeemed immortal cell,
          to enter paradise.
Now with the tide receding, I foretell
          I'll never reach my goal,
     although I still cannot conceive
that nothing living will descend from me.
          Through all the spume and roll
and slashing of the unrelenting waves,
     I hear a drowning fellow call:
"We are such stuff as dreams are made on" and
     I know at last that loss is all.

FALLING AWAY

And when I looked you slowly in the eye,
    I heard a pulsing in the wind,
        a pounding on the hill,
the water rising over lichened stones;
    huge heaving firs and hemlocks still
        concealed their owls as I
    came howling closer to the source
as from the cave old echoes spun and swirled
        and from the fire live colors
    broke apart and merged and whirled
        like comets through the night:
wild oranges that flared to yellow, flared to red,
    wild purples deepening to blue,
wild greens emerging from the diamond core.
        And as I entered you
with you enfolding me, not like the hunt,
    not with thick fury in my blood,
        but to explore and find
    where hungry lips had been before,
where murmured water sounds flowed through my mind.
    And having reached that holy place,
I knew it by its feel, which eased my heart
        and quieted my bones;
    I knew it with the certainty
of moonlight glistening on sacred stones
    through whose high arches we had tracked
        the pathways of the stars.
As if I'd never left, oh I could see,

with my eyes closed, the safety
of familiar dark, a dark without an enemy
            crouching behind a stump,
without the bared-tooth breathing in the brush—
        as if blind touch had taken on
the vividness of all things visible.
            And with distraction gone,
        I let my body be absorbed
in one encompassing sensation, one
            inclusive onward flow
        to where you were and were again,
to where I'd been and where I wished to go
            and go on still advancing
        in the long, remembering return
            as colors from the fire
        renewed themselves and tore apart
and merged again in their released desire
        that lit the bison on the wall
            and made them blink their eyes.
And there in that warm cave I wished to stay,
            but then I dimly heard
the echoed sound of waters fall away;
        I heard the wind turn inward
in the hemlock grove and disappear
            into the owl-hunched night,
and I woke open-eyed beyond the cave
        far in the woods, no fire in sight,
            without your whispered words,
        without your white glance fixed to mine
            like moonlight on a lake,
like sunlight beaming through a rifted cloud.
        All I could do, for my soul's sake,
            was save myself to find
another way to make the long return again,
        and so I waited, spear in hand,

silent as stone behind a hemlock stump,
    watching the wet lips of a band
of grazing bison as they raised their heads
    above the grasses on the plain,
      and when one fell behind,
I leapt out like a leopard in the chase,
    bison-blood blazing in my mind,
her taste anticipated on my tongue,
    and drove my trembling spear
into her side. I saw her spirit life
    spring from the steaming wound, look back,
and disappear, just as my skinning knife
    did what it was compelled to do.
      Before her twitching stopped
she turned her eyes to me as if to say
    she understood, but even then
I had already fallen far away,
    and I am falling farther still,
falling through fury of night winds that twist
    the agitated ferns,
beyond the border of familiar dark
    where late the lost pursuer turns.

CURING SLEEP

The Neanderthals were the first to bury their dead, the first to believe in an afterlife. Around the skeleton of a young man lay clusters of more than 2,000 grains of fossil pollen. One early summer day 60,000 years ago people had lain him to rest on a bed of yellow, white, and blue flowers, grape hyacinth, rose mallow, hollyhock, bachelor's button, groundsel. The flowers are or were believed to have healing powers.—John E. Pfeiffer, *The Creative Explosion*

Sleep well, young father; rest
in your belief that life renews itself
to breed an afterlife
in which upon a seeded bed of flowers
you'll be reunited with your wife,

your parents, children, dog—
yes, everything you've had brief time to love.
Conceiving death, your brain
has widened to experience what can't be seen,
to picture things that can't remain

remaining if you conjure them to sight:
grape hyacinth, rose mallow, groundsel,
hollyhocks, and bachelor's button—all
with power to restore
such losses in the sun that fall

into the darkness of your dreamless night.
Sleep well, and I will speak for you
the healing names your pale lips could not know
that early summer day
some sixty thousand years ago

to fill your patient waiting in the earth,
        to cure the hourless dark
    with colors that my waking mind
        offers thanksgiving for
in your behalf. My searching still can find

        groundsel for startled yellow,
grape hyacinth for englobed cerulean,
        for lavender or white,
    rose mallow in a glowing marsh,
or, by a roadside, bachelor's-button blue so bright

        it lights my passage home,
    though I absorb its glistening
before I move on to my garden bed
    where cultivated hollyhocks
that Nature made originally red

        flourish in new flamboyant hues!
Oh, we have given shape to planet Earth
        beyond your need's extreme
imagining, and we can heal such wounds
    that to your senses it might seem

we have transformed ourselves to gods.
    But we can't bring our loved dead back,
nor can we soften weeping in the night.
        You would be grieved to know
    how we've surpassed the raging might

of flood or fire or drought or parching winds
    or the obliterating snow
in our evolved capacity to kill;
        we have not learned to cure
the germ of murder replicating still

within us as the counterpart
of your invention of enduring paradise—
            as if to take a life
        fulfilled the passion not to die.
Sleep well; sleep on where no disease, no strife,

            no hunger of the heart
can touch you now among the elements,
        the simpler atoms of decay;
I'll tend my garden hours so what remains
        of your last wish won't blow away.

THE EMPTY THRONE

About 1230 B.C., Tukulti-Ninurta, tyrant of Assyria, had a stone altar made. In the carving Tukulti is shown twice, first as he approaches the throne of his god, and then as he kneels before it. The throne before which he grovels is empty. No king before in history is ever shown kneeling. No scene before in history ever indicates an absent god.—Julian Jaynes, *The Origin of Consciousness*

I watch myself attend Your throne
as if I were commanded to kneel there,
         but I've heard no command;
     where I'll go next I do not know
         since I can't understand
why You do not appear as You did
         in my father's reign.
I cannot rule without Your ruling me,
         for bone by sinewed bone,
You have created everything I am
         out of the speechless dust.
     You've given me the law so that
I judge, or I show mercy, as I must
         to satisfy Your wish
for glory in the city or the plains.
     I do not kill or burn
     unless I have Your word, and now,
without a promise that You will return,
         I watch myself imploring
     emptiness so vast, so high,
         it spreads out to the hills
and makes me ask myself which I is I—
     the standing I that witnesses
or the dazed I that kneels. And does another self
         watch my self watching there

with still another watcher watching that,
　　　and so on further into air
　　　　　as empty as the throne
　　　before my stony groveling?
Now everywhere I look, outside or in,
　　　blank swirling wind is circling me
but can't, beneath the serpent sun, begin
　　　to find an image of its own
to merge with on the unreflecting sand.
　　　I feel my thighs knot hard
before Your holy absence as I ask
　　　　　what penance I can do
　　　to cleanse my flesh, since I don't know
　　　　　what deed or thought of mine
　　　offended You? Perhaps I've hoarded
too much grain, taken too many concubines,
　　　or not provided gold enough
　　　　　inside my father's tomb.
I swear to that coiled serpent of the sun,
　　　I will renounce the world I find
　　　　　since I've already lost
myself in losing him, in losing You.
　　　It may be everything that once seemed
　　　　　solid in my mind
　　　has no more substance than a dew
upon an asphodel or on a spider's web,
　　　　　no more to worship as my own
than trickery of flickered candlelight
　　　that casts Your shadow on my throne.

AUTUMN BERRIES

You cannot hold the willow in your mind
    my brother said; you must
accept its vanishing—you must let go
    of Autumn's umber mellowness
while gazing on her brazen field. But no,
    red berries gleaming in the dew
        have blurred his warning voice
    and left me flushed and hungering
for more than parting's mood allows,
        mere wisps of heather
    waving by the marshy spring.
I wish my boldest golden willow wish
    to hold the season still,
to watch her berries shimmer in the dew
    before they wrinkle into rot,
to savor them, and to imagine you,
    resigning brother, ready to return
from dwelling in your barren land, to ask
    if I have lived the life I bet
my happiness upon, as if you learned
    my secret of regret,
that in my stubborn heart she has remained
    wild and desired and unpossessed,
the bounty of her berries in the morning light
    dissolving in the mist.

And still I try to hold her in my swirling sight
    so I can apprehend her berries
in their momentary glow, to marvel
      as their fullness fills to overfull.
But now with darkness coming over me,
        now in the interval
between her late arrival and the rush
     of my upsurging wish
    to savor those red berries in the dew
and keep her cloudy aura in the hills,
    as in my willow dream I do,
I see her figure vanishing; I see
    her shadowed meadow slope away.
       Perhaps, in timid haste,
she left her token by the willow when I looked,
     her hint that if I failed to taste
her berries, pleasure not experienced
    would sour my disbelieving blood
      and drive it through each vein
and harden fixed remorse into my skull
     whose grimace would remain
upon my gums and teeth to vindicate
    my brother's warning to *Let go*!
So who is she? What have I sought to feel,
    to hold, that now seems so remote
      yet palpably so real
in its elusiveness? Dressed in her purple hues,
    is she the beckoning projection
of my hunger's wish her ripeness cannot hide?
    Why, in this amber dawn,
when I have little left to harvest but my pride
    as chilled boughs stiffen in the trees,
     has she appeared again,
eternal in the instant of her vanishing?

And suddenly the field is hushed,
no crickets call, no drowsy wood doves sing,
   no winds carouse among the pines
or strum the thistle and the thorn; the dawn no longer
     is reflected in the dew,
and though red berries linger on my lips, I'm left,
   pale brother, here alone with you.

THREE

WITHIN MEASURE

for Nick Clifford

Mozart, you tell us, "Music
　　never should excite disgust,
and passions, whether violent or not,
　　　　must please the listener."
How terrible must life become before
　　　　music no longer can
　　transform disgust with art's relief?
What if the cure for violence requires
　　　　unmediated grief?
I picture you now playing your clavier
　　with no commission to fulfill,
just wandering at ease from key to key,
　　　　your improvising skill
　　at home in unrestricted time.
And looking down in an unmeasured lull
　　from such a cloudy eminence,
perhaps our snow-topped mountains seem as full
　　of evening's purple radiance
as you remember them; perhaps the oceans still
　　　　seem burgeoning with whales
all multiplying as designed in the beginning
　　　　as their plunging tails
compose white circles just to contemplate.
　　So, Mozart, from your height,
eternal music's heavenly remove,
　　you're mercifully spared the sight
of smothered birds clogged on oil-clotted shores,
　　of sulfur-saturated trees,

of ghostly radiation in the air,
        woodlands bulldozed to make way
for cement, the snarl of motors everywhere
    gnawing like locusts in a plague
to punish us for violation of the earth.
      The genius to destroy
    evolved with Mankind's upright stance:
we see our blight, and our infectious joy,
      which now our brain-child weapons
have made manifest, is to remove
      ourselves, redeem creation
so that less aggressive forms of life can prove
    their worthiness and multiply
without our usurpation of their space.
    Perhaps our violence evolved
      to cure us of ourselves;
perhaps atomic conflagration marks the last
    eruption of our first disease:
      our species' grinding past
of killing everything we look upon.
    And yet, apocalyptic judgment
in the mind can poison even our remorse!
    We need your music, Mozart; yes,
      we need your counter-force
that can console us with an old design
      of unpolluted seas:
accord of water and of lucid air
    to blend with the desire to please
      our fellow listeners.
I'll measure out wet wind upon the mountains
    of my mind to weep a lilting song;
beneath this cloud late healing music may
    remain for us to pass along.

THE DRAKE EQUATION

for Rich Wolfson

If Homo Sapiens owe their domination of Earth to their malevolent genius for violence, then our example suggests that. . . . advanced civilizations may be expected to self-destruct because they are in the destruction business; having lived by the sword, they die by the sword. . . . The Drake equation, $N = N^\star\ f_p\ n_e\ f_l\ f_i\ f_c\ L$, represents a thumbnail way of estimating the number of intelligent civilizations in the galaxy.—Timothy Ferris, *The Mind's Sky*

Assuming that catastrophe,
caused by our appetite to dominate,
            is fated by a star,
a sun like ours, because our destiny
        is manifest in what we are

            despite the best intent
        of some we know, should we not try
to pass along our species' memory
            of what we have achieved
        to others in the galaxy

who may be listening? If N stands for
        the number of societies
that might be eager to communicate,
        N asterisk in Drake's equation
            would be his fair estimate

        that some four hundred billion stars
are in the Milky Way; f_p assumes
            that roughly ten percent
have planets, which computes to forty billion, so
        if one in ten of these is meant

by Mother Nature to allow for cells
        to replicate and swarm
    and guard their space and fill the sea,
four billion planets might have life,
        which is the factor of n_e

adjusted by f_l. And if the chance against
        intelligence emerging is
        a hundredfold to one,
still forty million sun-warmed planets might
        already have begun

    to send radio signals out,
driven by their galactic loneliness,
        wishing to share, to see
        if someone else knows how thought feels;
that's calculated in f_i and in f_c.

    But now the most uncertain factor,
        final L, comes into play:
how long can technological societies survive
        before they lose control
        and manage blindly to contrive

their own annihilation? Thus, if L is small
        in evolutionary time—
look what swords have become in recent years!—
        then number N is low,
    which means it's likely that our deepest fears

    are true: power always corrupts,
and so-called civilized societies cannot
        last long enough to be in touch
        across the dusty night.
And yet, if ample L is not too much

for humankind to hope for as
survival based on peace,
on harmony with oceans, forests, sky—
though not on Earth our home,
but somewhere else that you and I

can dwell upon in thought—
it follows we must urge our fellow Drakians
to beam out to the waiting stars
beautiful conceptions
despite the torture and the wars:

Bach's Brandenburg Concertos and the melodies
Mozart invented to
give measure to the empty air, a pause
of sweet composure for the mind,
Euclid's geometry and Newton's laws

and Einstein's absolute—
both time and space are relative.
In spite of what we are, knowledge of these
must be preserved for someone
somewhere in our galaxy to seize

and contemplate and pass along,
so we can find some consolation here
and let the worst of what we've done
achieve obliteration
when our preyed-on Earth is swallowed by the sun.

THE BARBER OF CIVILITY

for Stanley Bates

We are asked to swallow a story about a village and a man in it who shaves all and only those men who [according to Lord Bertrand Russell's paradox] do not shave themselves. Grant this and we end up saying, absurdly, that the barber shaves himself if and only he does not. The proper conclusion to draw is just that there is no such barber.—W. V. O. Quine, *The Ways of Paradox*

Wishing to study the effects
    of bafflement, to see
if metaphysical uncertainty depressed
    or entertained a trusting mind,
Lord Russell's ghost appeared one night to test
    old Samson Horn, the tuneful barber
in my town, with his prize paradox:
    "Let's say a barber shaves all men
    who do not shave themselves;
accepting this, the problem for you, then,
    is to decide if you're allowed,
according to these rules, to shave yourself."
    Old Samson took these rules to heart,
    for one can't have, he reasoned,
    marriage, friendship, sports, or art
    without constraining forms;
yet opposite conclusions seemed to him
    logically inescapable,
nor was this splitting hairs—for if a barber
    does not shave himself, the full
import of his not doing so is that
    he's bound to shave himself;
and if he shaves before it's time for bed,
    the rules do not permit
    his taking scissors to his head.
Old Samson called and woke me from a nap

to cancel my appointment since
he could no longer work until he figured out
        what this strange civil war
in his divided soul was all about,
    although an operatic joy
            swelled up in him when logic
spurned itself—as if the world we see
        will not allow our words
to penetrate its silent mystery.
        Samson closed down his barbershop
                in the abandoned mill,
    and vanished with his cats and dogs,
            though I can see him still,
        his scissors poised above my head,
until a snip achieved perfection worthy
        of a Michelangelo.
            And I have kept my vow
from snow to rain and rain again to snow
        that I won't shave till he returns;
I walk the bridge as misty dawn swirls in,
            and wonder if he took
the ghost to be a sign that he begin
            another life in which
it's possible to shave and not to shave at once,
        to stay and to depart,
    to feel compassion with the mind
and follow algorithms with the heart.
        My beard is now so long
    that friends suspect some crisis changed
my image of myself, but that's absurd—
        although, on the warped barber sign,
look there! I see Lord Russell's ghost transformed—
            into a luminescent bird.

WITZELSUCHT

for John Bertolini

Witzelsucht—literally wit-seeking, characterized by "a morbid tendency to
pun and tell pointless stories while being inordinately entertained thereby."
—*Stedman's Medical Dictionary*

So if your melancholy spirit needs
      some pointless healing stories,
    hear me out, don't turn away;
not even Job, boiling with righteousness,
    has suffered more than I today,

plagued with a morbid tendency to tell
      inordinately rambling tales—
        that is my *pun*ishment—
    as Dante circled in his hell
the heretics whose disbelief had sent

    them howling to their burning doom
to verbalize forever the divinity
      they thought could not exist.
Our postlapsarian delight in speech
      arose because we missed

the slithing serpent's subtle badinage,
    original rebelliousness,
and thus blasphemers, like Caphaneus,
      who held God in disdain,
and whom the awestruck Dante shows to us

as unrelenting in his pride,
though tortured by his own revilings, still
      evoke our sympathy—
like rocked Prometheus who burned great Zeus
      with his discursive empathy

for humankind, or like the nonstop talker
      Milton falls for in his epic,
fork-tongued Satan's gift to lie and cheat
      so his orations might excel.
Dante describes the earthbound man of Crete:

      his head was fashioned of fine gold,
he had smooth silver arms, though to the waist
      he was composed of brass;
      one foot was iron, one was clay,
though Dante does not specify his balls or ass.

      He's meant to symbolize
the degradation of our race,
      the long decline of human history
that once enjoyed a golden age,
down to the current era of mined irony

      and double-duty puns,
and that demise is why he wept, his tears
      returning speechless to the ground.
Dante informs us that this human mountain, Crete,
      was where the goddess, Rhea, found

a place to hide her infant, Zeus, as told
      by Hesiod about cruel Kronos
who, in fear that he'd be overthrown,
      swallowed his children, though
his good wife Rhea fooled him with a stone,

which, wrapped in swaddling clothes,
got gulped down by deluded Kronos who
mistook the stone for Zeus his son.
Old Kronos could not stomach fate's decree;
he vomited and raged like one

provoked, like lecturing Achilles with his spear
who chased around the walls of Troy
ribbed Hector till he hit his own appointed sod
and got the final point:
don't mess with any offspring of a God!

This leads me back to wailing Job
who cursed God, knowing that defiant speech
was antidote to his despair,
or Hamlet who once thought it kosher to find
quarrel in a straw. Yes, anywhere

bold entertainment braves fate's odds to save
the gloomy from their somber gloom,
from feeling spent and spooked
and disinherited, split off as heirs, you'll find
the laureled ghost of *Witzelsucht.*

BONKERS

Bonkers, the half-tame deer, lost her freedom earlier this year after a jogger complained the doe was harassing him. She was deposited two weeks ago on isolated Savage Island, but took to the water and swam nearly two miles. Once ashore, Bonkers crashed a Fourth of July volleyball game, walked up to Ricky Irwin, licked his hand and ambled off.—*The Burlington Free Press, July 5th, 1987*

It's Independence Day—the band strikes up
    "God Bless America,"
and in Vermont the Peaceful Kingdom has begun
    its promised reign. Now, Ricky Irwin,
you have been anointed the named one
    Bonkers has chosen to receive
her message of our time-bound unity
    the instant that white volleyball
      is thrown up in the light,
so you can score the winning point—and all
    us gifted players, panting here,
pause in astonishment. Yes, Ricky, now we know,
    as Bonkers licks your hand
and momentary divine silence stuns
    the mundane music of the band,
      that revelation comes
quite unexpectedly. Time out is called
    and in a wink it's clear to you,
"They also serve who only stand and wait,"
    describes what's literally true
as you wait there, the ball in your licked hand.
    So God bless Bonkers; she alone
      has brought redeeming news
this day of deep dependence at the bone
    of creature-need to reach
across the fearful barriers of difference,

of color, gender, shape, or dress.
Although she lost her freedom
on the Savage Island of forced loneliness,
punished because some jogger,
locked in his routine, could find no use
for her companionship,
she swam two miles to interrupt our play
so she could free us from the grip
of our oblivion,
reminding us our sunlit planet must
be shared with birds, with trees,
with animals and plants and fish,
plankton meandering upon the seas.
We must take care or else our world's
chance balances, providing lungs with oxygen,
clear water for our thirst,
and romping images with which to dream,
break down to what they were at first,
dumbly inert and thus without the need
to be protected by
a cultivating human guardian.
The brawling game resumes,
the band picks up its brassy beat again
as Bonkers blithely ambles off
as if no revelation has occurred,
so we resume our play,
blessed by the spirit of a holiday,
before we must return
to our own ordinary lives.
And now, with Bonkers gone,
it seems lulled Nature loosed upon the land
some random kookiness
we do not have the talent yet to understand.

MY DISTANT FRIEND

"We've only been around
for 50,000 years," I tell my guest
from our adjoining galaxy,
"that's all we needed to contrive to blow
our planet from its orbit
in a—step right up and watch!—stupendous show
of mock divinity,
accomplishing what dinosaurs could not,
despite their bulk, achieve before,
because they lacked intelligence sufficient
to conceive of global war."
"This once upon a planetary lifetime feat,
can such an end be coming true?"
my friend inquires,
who's stopping here while passing through
to his own planet where the folk are self-aware
and yet not death-obsessed.
"Good riddance!" he blurts out so gruffly
that I wince, "to life descended from a fang,
not smart enough to change at heart."
I know my shocked friend meant
no harm to me; perhaps just being near
our species makes him violent
since we remind him of *his* species' past
before they took their canine genes,
their DNA, in hand, and redesigned
themselves as herbivores.
"We'd gone as far as our old hunting mind

allowed for us to go together
in our given space," he says, "of numbered trees
within our fragile atmosphere
returning water free of acid wastes
like yours, fragrant and clear,
good water that won't strangle what it breeds.
And we transformed desire
to dominate and to possess
into our worshiping the fertile color green,
until at death, as you might guess,
we are what we have thrived upon, and we
diminish into seeds
regenerating to the ground."
I listened to his softened voice and felt a pang
of anger toward our human kind
that won't let fortune linger in the sun
where blessing first was found.
"Let be your rivers!" he exclaims,
"let be your woodlands and your air, but not the crime
you poisoners commit
upon your planetary home."
As he moves closer I
am tempted to suspect from my friend's smile
he secretly approves
our species' self-appointed end
before we propagate
his world and, unreformed at heart, repeat
our fury and our hate.
And yet I looked out at our acid air,
our trees' degraded green,
and heard my friend's farewell "Let be!"
still trembling there.

DETERMINATION

Lost brother, having died the summer death
    I might have died, by your own hand,
        stilled heart within my heart,
    if I assume even my words
have been determined as the cosmic laws
        required right from the start,
including my hypothesis today
    that I'm determined also
to believe determination is the way
        fixed nature operates,
    from quarks to quandaries of the mind,
from numbing gloom to stoic pride,
        how can I ever know
    if what I think is true is true,
despite my best determination to decide?
        How can I ever know,
    strolling along the breeding lake
that we explored when we were boys, searching
        for turtles sunning on their rocks,
        for frogs, a water snake,
if my return can free me from the day
        you took your shadowed silence with you
        and you stole away.
And if I could return in time as well,
        even with what I know,
    in thought I'd choose again to be
the same abandoned boy I was—although
        he led me where I am today,

hearing across the lake the crack of ice,
    which brings back that same summer dawn
        you rose from our twin bed,
    without a parting word to me,
and put that silver pistol to your head.
    Why you? More inward than I was,
still, I believed, you loved the orange light
    that curled at evening in the pines,
the quick cry of the scarlet tanager,
    the congregating goldenrod
        and purple aster, signs
    of coming autumn's fierce effulgence
in the forest and the hills; you loved
    the pulsing northern lights, the sense
        of spectacle revealing
there is only spectacle to be revealed—
    profusion streaming in the sky,
profusion flowing golden in the field.
    So why did flashing colors,
flaring purple, flaring red, the oranges,
    the blues and greens and yellows—
        anyone who looks can see
    swirling the heavens and the earth—
that brought such thoughtless happiness to me,
    with no need for a purpose past
        appearing to be watched
    for sudden red or drizzling gray
transforming into brightened shades of blue—
    why, silent brother, in the last
accounting did such spectacle of color not
    bring equal happiness to you?
Was it too difficult to look out there
    into a universe that seemed
content to be exactly as it was?
    Given your inwardness, I fear

your death was unavoidable, and yet
        if dad had never brought
    that pistol home, and I, so late
to use it, left it in its cabinet, or tried
    to say what I could not have said,
            could I have changed your fate?
You put that shining pistol to your head,
    determined you would live your death
            as your own act of choice,
as if your ingrown silence could at last release
    locked words long stifled in my voice.

PICNIC WITH PARADOX

Let me assume, my dear, that justice will
          be done in the next life,
      that what I suffer here in this
polluted world will be rewarded with
      abundant compensating bliss
          of my own choosing—
      whether food or sex or walks
beside a silver stream, identifying birds,
          or philosophic talks
with god, who also loves a paradox.
          But if I know for sure
      that justice triumphs in the end,
          despite our human wars,
      despite betrayals and the loss
of animals and trees and parents, friends,
          then that benign belief
should bring me happiness in life and send
      my wishes back to where I am,
content in this bereaving world. Yet if
          I'm happy in this life
because I think that I'll be happy in the next,
      I won't, according to the rules
          of my own guiding text,
still qualify for compensating bliss
      in paradise: for champagne picnics
with slow kisses in a clover field,
          and thus without eternity
to hopefully anticipate, I'm trapped

again in mortal misery.
It seems my faith that compensating justice
     will be done is only true
          if I believe it's false,
          and if I still believe it's true—
a prophecy that floods me now with joy
          that I can share with you—
     then justice, in effect, already
          has been done on earth,
     and you and I can stroll along
some clear June day beside a dwindling stream,
     a picnic basket on my arm,
          young, confident, and strong,
     no need to fantasize or dream
as my uncontemplating body savors
     its own sun-warmed ecstasy.
But that depicted youthful me is not
          now who I am; that me is as
remote as paradise hypothesized,
     and you, how clearly I can see
          your vanished radiance
     that once made my unwary body
          blissfully oblivious
to anyone's distracting paradox.
     There was no need then to imagine
          there might come a day
when I'd be strolling by a silver stream,
     discussing justice with a god
          who oversees the way
     we struggle to make sense of suffering
or finally allows our memories to fade
     until thought is a glimpsed white bird
that disappears into the leafy shade
     without a lilting melody
          to recognize him by,
without a hopeful word, without a cry.

ELEGY TO THE SUN

Before diminishing into a cool *white dwarf*,
　　　five billion years from now
our home sun will explode and then turn red
　　　into a giant star. Though not my time,
it's true, it's time that lives inside my head,
　　　time my clenched heart can comprehend.
Because I'm tempted, I admit, to harbor
　　　　　personal offense,
　　　imagining her red change brings
apocalypse; it makes consoling sense
　　　to blame someone who's not to blame
so I'm not driven to review defeats
　　　and losses that depleted me.
These losses are so palpable I see
　　　them still before my eyes as if
　　　they were avoidable,
　　　as if my muse could be made young,
waving her white hat in the cherry tree
　　　where I encountered her among
such vast profusion of ripe fruit it seemed
　　　the cosmos was contained
within my poem that painted her in place.
　　　She held a cherry with her teeth,
sucked in, spat out the pit, and on her face
　　　a burst of cherry juice appeared,
which all my leafy greens and windy blues
　　　　could not accommodate.
There seethed more red than I had gray for rock,
　　　more red than I could dominate

with all the urgency of art that strives
       to hold what can't be held.
And as her image burned away, consumed
       by fiercer red, I felt compelled
              to cry out in earth colors
I could make my own, a rainstorm surge
       in ploughed-up brown and misty gray.
I filled the cherry tree with spectral pits
       where fruit once was, and brushed midday
              not into moonlit night,
but into pallor I remembered from
       one summer sun's silent eclipse,
              a white so eerie cold
       it formed the cry, *white*, on my lips,
which frosted in the leaves as one by one
       I tinted them. Yet in that white
more white was deepening, white of the polar snows,
              white of the tropic seas,
       white of a mind that knows
it knows the ultimate, effulgent flare of red,
       the anger at the end, the withdrawn hand
              of dazed, dumbfounded art
       that feels betrayed by what it touched
and yet could not possess—as if loss were the part
       nature dares us to cherish most.
But with our sun's end whitened in my mind,
       loss ceases to seem personal,
              and so the cherry tree
resumes its ripening and its decay, the full
       not yet exhausted cycling
destined to complete itself. There sits my muse,
       reposing higher in the tree,
waving her white straw hat at someone else
       who in this orange evening light,
shading toward red, she might mistake for me.

THE TREES WILL DIE

An increase of one degree in average temperature moves the climatic zones
thirty-five to fifty miles north. . . . The trees will die. Consider nothing more
than that—just that the trees will die.—Bill McKibben, *The End of Nature*

Late in Vermont let me consider
some familiar trees I've lived among
for thirty years of sleet and snow,
of sun and rain: the aspens
quaking silver when the wet winds blow,

the white oaks, with their seven-lobed leaves
and gently furrowed bark,
whose April buds sprout reddish-brown;
and I'll consider pin oaks,
their stiff branches sloping down

asserting their own space, and sculpted leaves,
flaming vermilion in the fall,
holding on even when they're curled and dry,
through freezing winter storms
in which we huddle, you and I,

around a fire that woos us back to feel
what our ancestors felt
some sixty thousand years ago;
and I'll consider red oaks with their pointed leaves,
shiny dark trunks that seem to know

the secret of slow growth,
a message safe to pass along.
And then, considering the plenitude
of maples here, I'll start with sugar
for its syrup and its symmetry, its brood

of tiny yellow flower clusters
in the spring, and in the autumn such a blaze
of orange, gold, and red,
whatever gloom might form the drizzling weather
in my doom-reflecting head,

relief comes from the self-forgetfulness
of looking at what's there—
the trees, the multitude of trees.
I stop here to consider in the brief years left
to praise them and to please

you who have loved their scented shade,
their oceanic choiring in the wind. And so I'll list
a few more that I know:
the silver maple and the willow and the birch,
box elder, basswood, and the shadblow

whose pinkish-white flowers
quicken the awakened woods
and quicken me. And then the spruce and pines,
their slender, tapered cones
glimmering intricate designs

that tempt astonished eyes to contemplate
how an indifferent force—
just evolutionary randomness,
yet so like old divinity—
could wrest such pattern from initial emptiness.

Before our history began,
        the void commanded
there be congregated trees and creatures filled
        with words to mimic them
        and represent the moods that spilled

out of the creature's thoughts into the world
        so that the trees and names for trees
            would then be joined as one:
the melancholy hemlocks in the humming dark,
        the tamaracks which flare gold in the sun

            as if to hold the light
of wavering October in their arms
        a little longer, as I do—
yet though they're evergreens at heart,
            like me, my dear, and you,

they lose their needles when the cold comes on.
        And as the tilted planet turns
to offer us fresh colors that embellish speech,
        more names rush into view:
the sycamore, the cedar, and the beech,

            horse chestnut, butternut,
the hickories, black walnut, and of course
        the cornucopia of fruits—
apple and cherry, pear and plum and peach—
            each with a tang that suits

        the palate of whatever taste
one might have dreamed of ripened paradise.
        When I consider how
a man-made shift in climate of a few degrees
        reveals the rebel power we now

        have learned to cultivate
in order to subdue the animals
        and take dominion, like a curse,
over the fields, the forests, and the atmosphere—
                as if the universe

        belonged to us alone—I wonder
if consideration of the family of trees
        might give us pause
and let us once again obey the sun,
        whose light commands all human laws.